D0325680

Dear Jane

Dear Jane

WISE COUNSEL FROM

MS. AUSTEN AND FRIENDS

Clarkson Potter/Publishers

NEW YORK

CLARKSON POTTER is a trademark and POTTER with colophon
is a registered trademark of Penguin Random House LLC.

ISBN 978-0-451-49573-0

Printed in China

Book design by La Tricia Watford
Illustrations by Shutterstock/Kotkoa
Cover design by La Tricia Watford
Text by Emma Brodie

10 9 8 7 6 5 4 3 2 1

First Edition

For Jane
and all the headstrong females
who love her

ETIQUETTE & LIFESTYLE

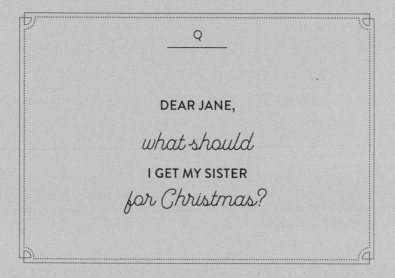

Q

DEAR JANE,

what should
I GET MY SISTER
for Christmas?

A

NOBODY MINDS HAVING WHAT IS
too good for them.

—*JANE AUSTEN*
MANSFIELD PARK, 1814

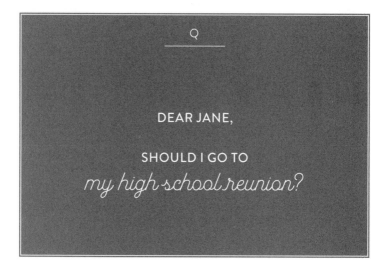

Q

DEAR JANE,

SHOULD I GO TO
my high school reunion?

A
___

PERFECT HAPPINESS,

even in memory,

IS NOT COMMON.

—*JANE AUSTEN*
EMMA, 1815

Q
_____

DEAR JANE,

I FEEL LIKE I'M GETTING TOO OLD
to throw a birthday bash,
BUT I STILL WANT TO. SHOULD I?

A
_____

one cannot have

TOO LARGE A PARTY.

—JANE AUSTEN
EMMA, 1815

Q
———

DEAR JANE,

ARE THERE ANY CONVERSATION TOPICS
I should generally avoid
IN MIXED COMPANY?

A
_____

from politics.

IT [I]S AN EASY STEP TO SILENCE.

—*JANE AUSTEN*
NORTHANGER ABBEY, 1818

Q

DEAR JANE,

compliments make me

REALLY UNCOMFORTABLE.

how can I avoid them?

A

YOU MUST TRY NOT TO
mind growing up
INTO A PRETTY WOMAN.

—*JANE AUSTEN*
MANSFIELD PARK, 1814

Q
———

DEAR JANE,

now that we're married,

IS IT COOL IF I GET RID OF

my husband's futon?

A

marriage indeed

IS A MANEUVERING BUSINESS.

—JANE AUSTEN

MANSFIELD PARK, 1814

Q
_____

DEAR JANE,

MY BROTHER GOT ME

a pogo stick for Christmas.

WTF?

A

WHAT STRANGE CREATURES
brothers are!

—*JANE AUSTEN*
MANSFIELD PARK, 1814

Q

DEAR JANE,

SHOULD I REALLY

buy multiples

WHEN I FIND A PRODUCT I LIKE?

A

IT IS WELL TO HAVE

as many holds

UPON HAPPINESS AS POSSIBLE.

—JANE AUSTEN
EMMA, 1815

Q
___

DEAR JANE,

AM I COLDHEARTED IF I CAN'T
stand Valentine's Day?

A
_____

THERE ARE AS MANY FORMS OF LOVE

as there are moments in time.

—*JANE AUSTEN*
LETTERS, 1932

DEAR JANE,

I'm going to a wedding
AND I CAN'T TELL FROM THE INVITE
how formal it is.
WHAT SHOULD I WEAR?

A

one had rather,

ON SUCH OCCASIONS,

DO TOO MUCH THAN TOO LITTLE.

—*JANE AUSTEN*
SENSE AND SENSIBILITY, 1811

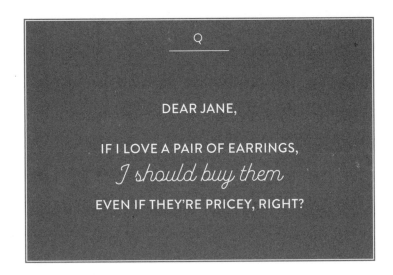

Q

DEAR JANE,

IF I LOVE A PAIR OF EARRINGS,
I should buy them
EVEN IF THEY'RE PRICEY, RIGHT?

A
___

how quick come the reasons

FOR APPROVING WHAT WE LIKE!

–JANE AUSTEN

PERSUASION, 1817

continues ➤➤

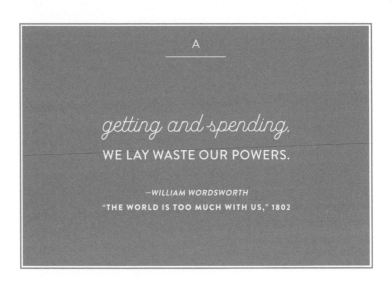

A

getting and spending,
WE LAY WASTE OUR POWERS.

—WILLIAM WORDSWORTH
"THE WORLD IS TOO MUCH WITH US," 1802

A

---

oh!

WHAT A TANGLED WEB

we weave.

—SIR WALTER SCOTT

MARMION, 1808

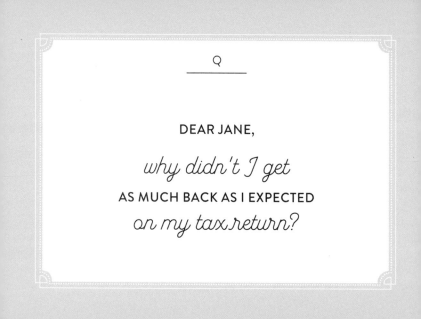

Q
———

DEAR JANE,

why didn't I get

AS MUCH BACK AS I EXPECTED

on my tax return?

A

THOSE WHO HAVE NOT MORE,
must be satisfied with
WHAT THEY HAVE.

—*JANE AUSTEN*
MANSFIELD PARK, 1814

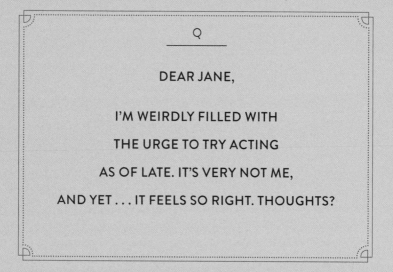

Q

DEAR JANE,

I'M WEIRDLY FILLED WITH
THE URGE TO TRY ACTING
AS OF LATE. IT'S VERY NOT ME,
AND YET . . . IT FEELS SO RIGHT. THOUGHTS?

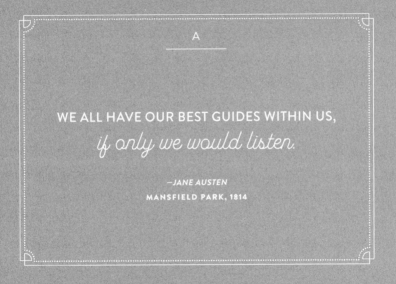

A

WE ALL HAVE OUR BEST GUIDES WITHIN US,
if only we would listen.

—*JANE AUSTEN*
MANSFIELD PARK, 1814

CAREER

Q

DEAR JANE,

how do I

FIND A FULFILLING CAREER?

A
_____

YOU WANT NOTHING BUT PATIENCE—

OR GIVE IT A MORE FASCINATING NAME,

CALL IT HOPE.

—JANE AUSTEN
SENSE AND SENSIBILITY, 1811

Q
_____

DEAR JANE,

TODAY I BOMBED A PRESENTATION.

how can I face my

COWORKERS AGAIN?

A

for what do we live,
BUT TO MAKE SPORT FOR OUR NEIGHBORS
and laugh at them in our turn?

—*JANE AUSTEN*
PRIDE AND PREJUDICE, 1813

Q
_____

DEAR JANE,

MY COWORKER JUST TOOK
credit for my idea.
SHOULD I STAND UP FOR MYSELF
or let it lie?

A
_____

let your conduct

BE THE ONLY HARANGUE.

—JANE AUSTEN

MANSFIELD PARK, 1814

Q
————

DEAR JANE,

HOW SHOULD I HANDLE IT
WHEN I DON'T AGREE
WITH MY BOSS?

A
_____

in nine cases out of ten,
A WOMAN HAD BETTER SHOW MORE
affection than she feels.

—*JANE AUSTEN*
PRIDE AND PREJUDICE, 1813

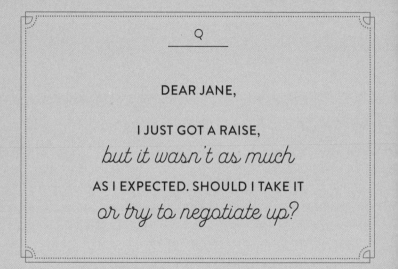

Q

DEAR JANE,

I JUST GOT A RAISE,
but it wasn't as much
AS I EXPECTED. SHOULD I TAKE IT
or try to negotiate up?

A

if a woman doubts

AS TO WHETHER SHE SHOULD

accept a man or not,

SHE CERTAINLY OUGHT TO REFUSE HIM.

—*JANE AUSTEN*
EMMA, 1815

Q

DEAR JANE,

HOW DO I COME UP
with a good idea?

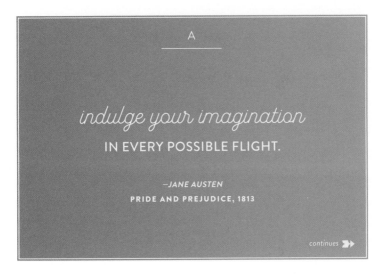

A

indulge your imagination

IN EVERY POSSIBLE FLIGHT.

—*JANE AUSTEN*

PRIDE AND PREJUDICE, 1813

continues ⏵⏵

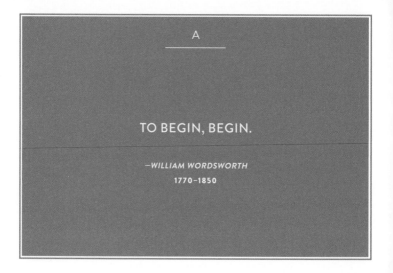

A

TO BEGIN, BEGIN.

—*WILLIAM WORDSWORTH*
1770–1850

A

the will to do,

THE SOUL TO DARE.

—*SIR WALTER SCOTT*
1771–1832

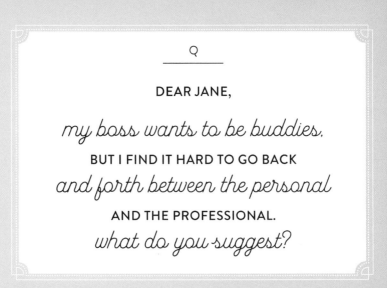

Q
_____

DEAR JANE,

my boss wants to be buddies,
BUT I FIND IT HARD TO GO BACK
and forth between the personal
AND THE PROFESSIONAL.
what do you suggest?

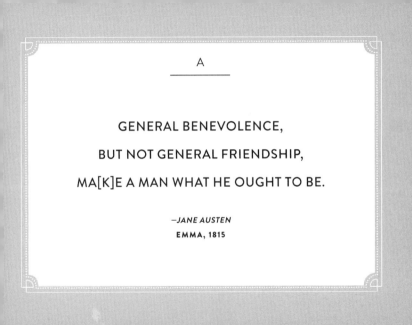

A
———

GENERAL BENEVOLENCE,

BUT NOT GENERAL FRIENDSHIP,

MA[K]E A MAN WHAT HE OUGHT TO BE.

—*JANE AUSTEN*
EMMA, 1815

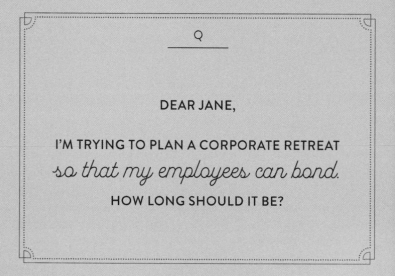

Q
_____

DEAR JANE,

I'M TRYING TO PLAN A CORPORATE RETREAT
so that my employees can bond.
HOW LONG SHOULD IT BE?

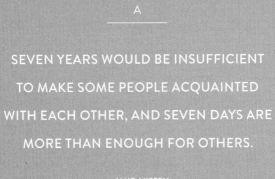

A

SEVEN YEARS WOULD BE INSUFFICIENT
TO MAKE SOME PEOPLE ACQUAINTED
WITH EACH OTHER, AND SEVEN DAYS ARE
MORE THAN ENOUGH FOR OTHERS.

—JANE AUSTEN
SENSE AND SENSIBILITY, 1811

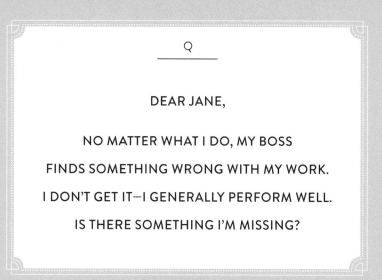

DEAR JANE,

NO MATTER WHAT I DO, MY BOSS
FINDS SOMETHING WRONG WITH MY WORK.
I DON'T GET IT—I GENERALLY PERFORM WELL.
IS THERE SOMETHING I'M MISSING?

A

WHERE THERE IS A DISPOSITION

to dislike,

A MOTIVE WILL NEVER BE WANTING.

—JANE AUSTEN
LADY SUSAN, 1871

Q

DEAR JANE,

I WANT TO MAKE GREAT ART,
but I don't want to be a
"MISERABLE ARTIST."
is that possible?

A

let other pens

DWELL ON GUILT AND MISERY.

—JANE AUSTEN

MANSFIELD PARK, 1814

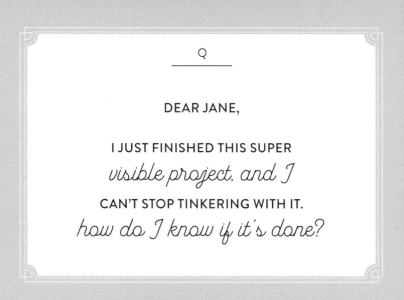

Q

DEAR JANE,

I JUST FINISHED THIS SUPER *visible project, and I* CAN'T STOP TINKERING WITH IT. *how do I know if it's done?*

A
———

OH! WRITE, WRITE. FINISH IT AT ONCE.

LET THERE BE AN END

OF THIS SUSPENSE.

FIX, COMMIT, CONDEMN YOURSELF.

—JANE AUSTEN
MANSFIELD PARK, 1814

Q

DEAR JANE,

I JUST LOST AN

entire powerpoint presentation,

WHAT IF I GET FIRED?

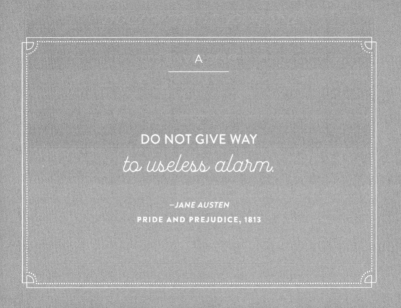

A

DO NOT GIVE WAY

to useless alarm.

—JANE AUSTEN
PRIDE AND PREJUDICE, 1813

FRIENDSHIP

Q

DEAR JANE,

my roommate is mad

BECAUSE I BORROWED HER SWEATER.

what's the big deal?

A

silly things do cease to be silly

IF THEY ARE DONE BY SENSIBLE PEOPLE

in an impudent way.

—JANE AUSTEN

EMMA, 1815

Q

DEAR JANE,

HOW DO I TELL MY ROOMMATE

her plant died

WHILE SHE WAS ON VACATION?

A

I WILL NOT SAY THAT YOUR

mulberry-trees are dead,

BUT I AM AFRAID THEY ARE NOT ALIVE.

—JANE AUSTEN
LETTERS, 1932

Q

DEAR JANE,

my roommate is unfriendly

WHENEVER I HAVE PEOPLE OVER.

what gives?

A

there are some people

WHO CANNOT BEAR A PARTY OF PLEASURE.

—*JANE AUSTEN*
SENSE AND SENSIBILITY, 1811

Q
_____

DEAR JANE,

EVERY TIME I BURN INCENSE,
my roommate acts weird.
IF I DIDN'T KNOW BETTER, I'D SAY
she's annoyed.

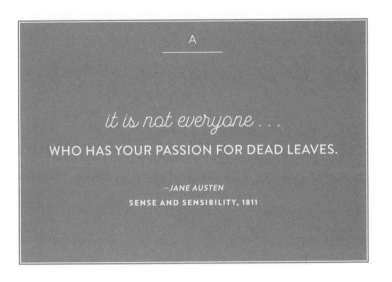

A

it is not everyone . . .

WHO HAS YOUR PASSION FOR DEAD LEAVES.

—JANE AUSTEN
SENSE AND SENSIBILITY, 1811

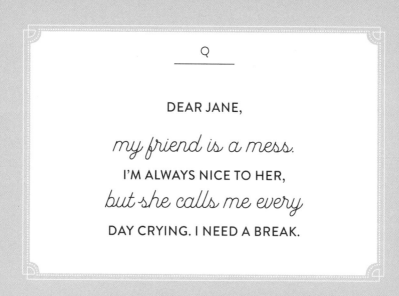

Q

DEAR JANE,

my friend is a mess.
I'M ALWAYS NICE TO HER,
but she calls me every
DAY CRYING. I NEED A BREAK.

A
___

there are people,
WHO THE MORE YOU DO FOR THEM,
the less they will do
FOR THEMSELVES.

—JANE AUSTEN
EMMA, 1815

Q
___

DEAR JANE,

my friend just made a really

UNCHARACTERISTICALLY CUTTING COMMENT.

could that be what

SHE REALLY THINKS?

A

_____

seldom can it happen that
SOMETHING IS NOT A LITTLE DISGUISED,
or a little mistaken.

—*JANE AUSTEN*
EMMA, 1815

Q
____

DEAR JANE,

I LOVE MY FRIEND,

BUT WHENEVER WE GO OUT SHE ACTS LIKE

IT'S A COMPETITION FOR MALE ATTENTION.

WHAT HAPPENED TO MATES BEFORE DATES?

A

[SHE] IS ONE OF THOSE YOUNG LADIES
WHO SEEK TO RECOMMEND THEMSELVES
TO THE OTHER SEX BY UNDERVALUING THEIR
OWN . . . IN MY OPINION, IT IS A
PALTRY DEVICE, A VERY MEAN ART.

—JANE AUSTEN
PRIDE AND PREJUDICE, 1813

Q

DEAR JANE,

my best friend is moving away

FOR A YEAR. I'M SO SAD!

A

THERE IS NOTHING SO BAD
as parting with one's friends.
ONE SEEMS SO FORLORN WITHOUT THEM.

—*JANE AUSTEN*
PRIDE AND PREJUDICE, 1813

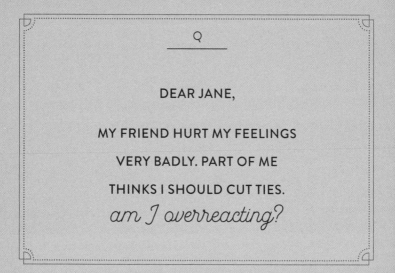

Q

DEAR JANE,

MY FRIEND HURT MY FEELINGS
VERY BADLY. PART OF ME
THINKS I SHOULD CUT TIES.
am I overreacting?

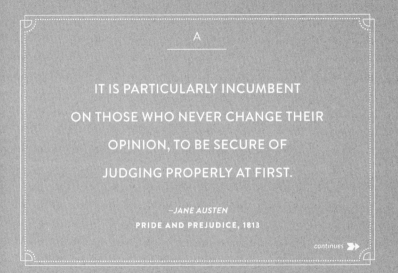

A

IT IS PARTICULARLY INCUMBENT
ON THOSE WHO NEVER CHANGE THEIR
OPINION, TO BE SECURE OF
JUDGING PROPERLY AT FIRST.

–JANE AUSTEN
PRIDE AND PREJUDICE, 1813

continues ▶▶

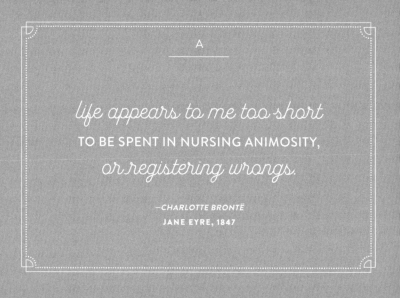

A

life appears to me too short
TO BE SPENT IN NURSING ANIMOSITY,
or registering wrongs.

—*CHARLOTTE BRONTË*
JANE EYRE, 1847

IN A DRAMA OF THE HIGHEST ORDER

there is little food for censure

OR HATRED; IT TEACHES RATHER

self-knowledge and self-respect.

—*PERCY BYSSHE SHELLEY*
"A DEFENSE OF POETRY," 1821

Q

DEAR JANE,

my friend's boyfriend broke up WITH HER WHILE SHE WAS VISITING ME. *now she will never want* TO VISIT ME AGAIN.

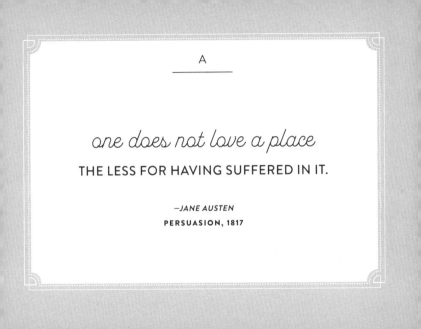

A

one does not love a place

THE LESS FOR HAVING SUFFERED IN IT.

—*JANE AUSTEN*

PERSUASION, 1817

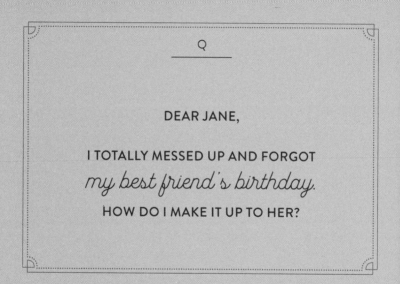

Q

DEAR JANE,

I TOTALLY MESSED UP AND FORGOT

my best friend's birthday.

HOW DO I MAKE IT UP TO HER?

A
___

YOU HAVE ANOTHER LONG WALK

before you.

—*JANE AUSTEN*

EMMA, 1815

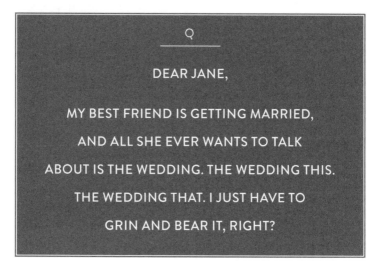

Q

DEAR JANE,

MY BEST FRIEND IS GETTING MARRIED,
AND ALL SHE EVER WANTS TO TALK
ABOUT IS THE WEDDING. THE WEDDING THIS.
THE WEDDING THAT. I JUST HAVE TO
GRIN AND BEAR IT, RIGHT?

A

HUMAN NATURE IS SO WELL DISPOSED

TOWARDS THOSE WHO ARE IN INTERESTING

SITUATIONS, THAT A YOUNG PERSON,

WHO EITHER MARRIES OR DIES, IS SURE OF

BEING KINDLY SPOKEN OF.

—JANE AUSTEN
EMMA, 1815

DATING

Q
_____

DEAR JANE,

I HAVE NOTHING TO WEAR
on my date tonight,
AND I'M FREAKING OUT!

A
———————

how often is happiness

DESTROYED BY PREPARATION,

foolish preparation!

—*JANE AUSTEN*

EMMA, 1815

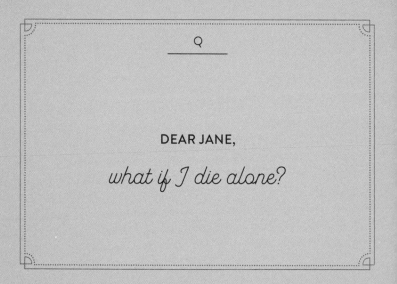

Q
——————

DEAR JANE,

what if I die alone?

A

WHEN A YOUNG LADY IS TO BE A HEROINE,
THE PERVERSENESS OF FORTY SURROUNDING
FAMILIES CANNOT PREVENT HER.
SOMETHING MUST AND WILL HAPPEN
TO THROW A HERO IN HER WAY.

—JANE AUSTEN
NORTHANGER ABBEY, 1818

Q

DEAR JANE,

SHOULD I TRY

Tinder?

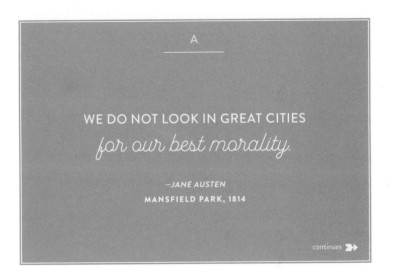

A

WE DO NOT LOOK IN GREAT CITIES
for our best morality.

—*JANE AUSTEN*
MANSFIELD PARK, 1814

continues ⇥

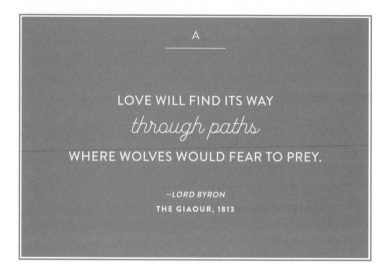

A

LOVE WILL FIND ITS WAY

through paths

WHERE WOLVES WOULD FEAR TO PREY.

—*LORD BYRON*
THE GIAOUR, 1813

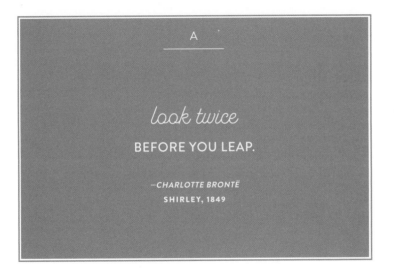

A

look twice

BEFORE YOU LEAP.

—*CHARLOTTE BRONTË*
SHIRLEY, 1849

DEAR JANE,

I HAD A SUMMER ROMANCE THAT
no one else can live up to
AND NONE OF MY FRIENDS
understand my pain.

A

_____

it was a delightful visit;

—PERFECT, IN BEING MUCH TOO SHORT.

—JANE AUSTEN

EMMA, 1815

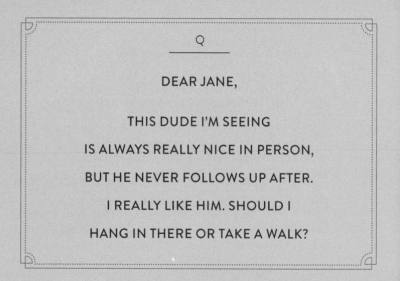

Q
_____

DEAR JANE,

THIS DUDE I'M SEEING
IS ALWAYS REALLY NICE IN PERSON,
BUT HE NEVER FOLLOWS UP AFTER.
I REALLY LIKE HIM. SHOULD I
HANG IN THERE OR TAKE A WALK?

A

WE ALL KNOW HIM TO BE A PROUD,
unpleasant sort of man;
BUT THIS WOULD BE NOTHING
if you really liked him.

—JANE AUSTEN
PRIDE AND PREJUDICE, 1813

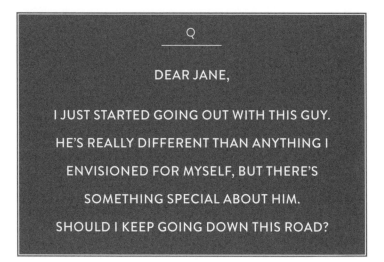

Q

DEAR JANE,

I JUST STARTED GOING OUT WITH THIS GUY.
HE'S REALLY DIFFERENT THAN ANYTHING I
ENVISIONED FOR MYSELF, BUT THERE'S
SOMETHING SPECIAL ABOUT HIM.
SHOULD I KEEP GOING DOWN THIS ROAD?

A

THERE IS HARDLY ANY PERSONAL DEFECT
which an agreeable manner
MIGHT NOT GRADUALLY RECONCILE ONE TO.

—JANE AUSTEN
PERSUASION, 1817

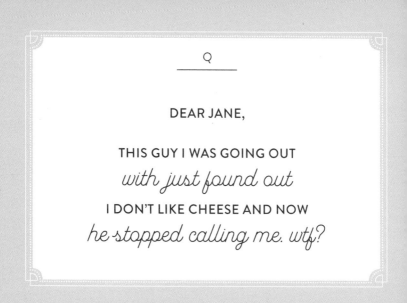

Q
_____

DEAR JANE,

THIS GUY I WAS GOING OUT
with just found out
I DON'T LIKE CHEESE AND NOW
he stopped calling me. wtf?

A
_____

SUCH SQUEAMISH YOUTHS AS

CANNOT BEAR TO BE CONNECTED WITH A LITTLE

ABSURDITY ARE NOT WORTH A REGRET.

—JANE AUSTEN
PRIDE AND PREJUDICE, 1813

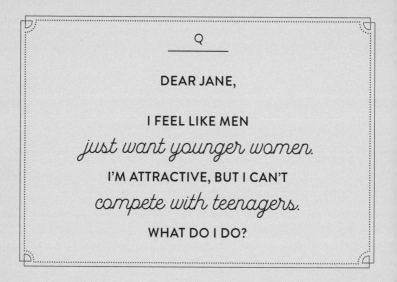

Q
___

DEAR JANE,

I FEEL LIKE MEN

just want younger women.

I'M ATTRACTIVE, BUT I CAN'T

compete with teenagers.

WHAT DO I DO?

A

it sometimes happens

THAT A WOMAN IS HANDSOMER

AT TWENTY-NINE THAN

she was ten years before.

—JANE AUSTEN
PERSUASION, 1817

Q

DEAR JANE,

IF A GUY TELLS ME I'M PRETTY,
that means he's falling
FOR ME, RIGHT?

A

it is very often nothing BUT OUR OWN VANITY THAT DECEIVES US. *women fancy admiration means* MORE THAN IT DOES.

—JANE AUSTEN
PRIDE AND PREJUDICE, 1813

continues ⏩

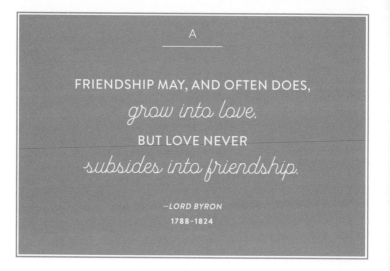

A

FRIENDSHIP MAY, AND OFTEN DOES,

grow into love,

BUT LOVE NEVER

subsides into friendship.

—LORD BYRON

1788–1824

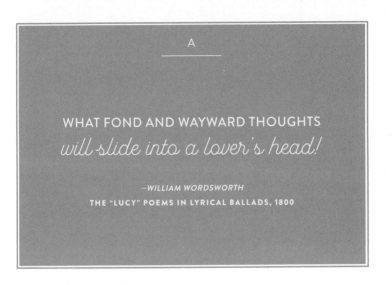

A

WHAT FOND AND WAYWARD THOUGHTS
will slide into a lover's head!

—WILLIAM WORDSWORTH
THE "LUCY" POEMS IN LYRICAL BALLADS, 1800

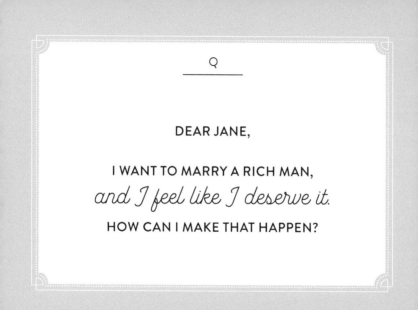

Q

DEAR JANE,

I WANT TO MARRY A RICH MAN,
and I feel like I deserve it.
HOW CAN I MAKE THAT HAPPEN?

A
_____

there certainly are not

SO MANY MEN OF LARGE FORTUNE

in the world as there are

PRETTY WOMEN TO DESERVE THEM.

—*JANE AUSTEN*

MANSFIELD PARK, 1814

Q

DEAR JANE,

WHY IS EVERYONE I MEET

a creeper?

A

STUPID MEN ARE THE ONLY ONES
worth knowing, after all.

—*JANE AUSTEN*
PRIDE AND PREJUDICE, 1813

Q

DEAR JANE,

I JUST STARTED DATING THIS GUY

who seems really great . . .

EXCEPT HE DOESN'T READ.

is that a deal breaker?

A

the person,

BE IT GENTLEMAN OR LADY, WHO HAS

not pleasure in a good novel,

MUST BE INTOLERABLY STUPID.

—JANE AUSTEN
NORTHANGER ABBEY, 1818

Q

DEAR JANE,

THIS GUY I JUST MET HAS TOTALLY
SWEPT ME OFF MY FEET. HE'S SO CUTE AND
SMART AND HE DOESN'T KNOW HOW CUTE
AND SMART HE IS. IS HE TOO GOOD TO BE TRUE?

A

NOTHING IS MORE DECEITFUL
than the appearance of humility.
IT IS OFTEN ONLY CARELESSNESS OF OPINION,
and sometimes an indirect boast.

—JANE AUSTEN
PRIDE AND PREJUDICE, 1813

continues ➼

A

those faces

WHICH HAVE CHARMED US MOST

escape us the soonest.

—*SIR WALTER SCOTT*
THE BETROTHED, 1825

A

NOTHING WILTS FASTER
than laurels that have
BEEN RESTED UPON.

—*PERCY BYSSHE SHELLEY*
1792–1822

Q

DEAR JANE,

THE GUY I'M DATING HASN'T
texted me back in seven hours.
IS HE GHOSTING ON ME?

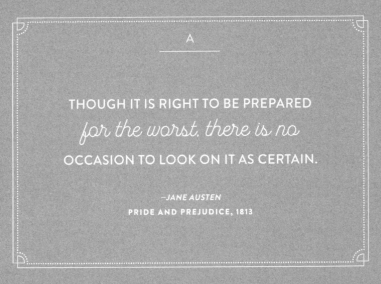

A

THOUGH IT IS RIGHT TO BE PREPARED
for the worst, there is no
OCCASION TO LOOK ON IT AS CERTAIN.

—JANE AUSTEN
PRIDE AND PREJUDICE, 1813

Q

DEAR JANE,

I THOUGHT THIS GUY REALLY LIKED ME,
BUT I GUESS NOT BECAUSE HE
JUST SAID HE WANTS TO SEE OTHER PEOPLE.
I'M SO BUMMED.

A

IF THE FIRST CALCULATION IS WRONG,

we make a second better:

WE FIND COMFORT SOMEWHERE.

—*JANE AUSTEN*
MANSFIELD PARK, 1814

Q

DEAR JANE,

WHAT SHOULD I LOOK FOR
in a partner?

there is no charm

EQUAL TO TENDERNESS OF HEART.

—*JANE AUSTEN*

EMMA, 1815

continues ▶▶

A
———

THE FLOWER OF SWEETEST SMELL

is shy and lowly.

—*WILLIAM WORDSWORTH*
"NOT LOVE, NOT WAR, NOR THE TUMULTUOUS SWELL," 1823

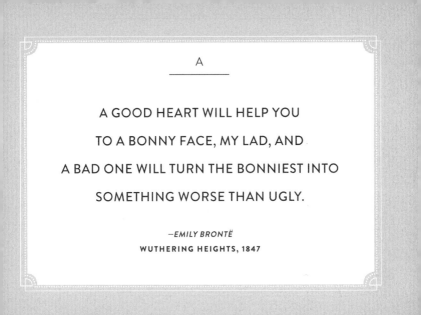

A

A GOOD HEART WILL HELP YOU
TO A BONNY FACE, MY LAD, AND
A BAD ONE WILL TURN THE BONNIEST INTO
SOMETHING WORSE THAN UGLY.

—*EMILY BRONTË*
WUTHERING HEIGHTS, 1847

Q

DEAR JANE,

WHAT'S THE BEST WAY

to meet eligible dudes?

A

TO BE FOND OF DANCING

was a certain step

TOWARDS FALLING IN LOVE.

—JANE AUSTEN
PRIDE AND PREJUDICE, 1813

Q
_____

DEAR JANE,

I'VE BEEN GOING OUT WITH THIS GUY.
HE'S REALLY NICE, BUT THERE'S NO SPARK.
WHEN IS THE RIGHT TIME TO TELL HIM
I'M NOT INTO IT?

A

what is right to be done

CANNOT BE DONE TOO SOON.

—JANE AUSTEN

EMMA, 1815

Q
———————

DEAR JANE,

NONE OF MY FRIENDS

like my boyfriend.

IS THAT A RED FLAG?

A

WHERE AN OPINION IS GENERAL,

it is usually correct.

—JANE AUSTEN

MANSFIELD PARK, 1814

Q

DEAR JANE,

I'VE BEEN SEEING THIS GUY FOR A WHILE.
WE'RE NOT IN A RELATIONSHIP . . . EXACTLY.
IT WAS FINE AT FIRST, BUT NOW I WANT
TO BE WITH HIM FOR REAL. IS IT WORTH
TRYING TO CHANGE THINGS?

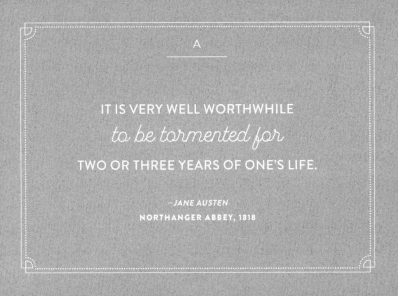

A

IT IS VERY WELL WORTHWHILE
to be tormented for
TWO OR THREE YEARS OF ONE'S LIFE.

—*JANE AUSTEN*
NORTHANGER ABBEY, 1818

Q

DEAR JANE,

THIS GUY I'VE BEEN SEEING BLOWS *really hot and cold. should I* ACCEPT HIS SELFISH BEHAVIOR BECAUSE *he's nice the rest of the time?*

A

SELFISHNESS MUST ALWAYS BE

forgiven you know,

BECAUSE THERE IS NO HOPE OF A CURE.

—JANE AUSTEN
MANSFIELD PARK, 1814

RELATIONSHIPS

Q

DEAR JANE,

I'M SCARED OF FALLING IN LOVE
and getting hurt.

A
_____

WE ARE ALL APT TO EXPECT TOO MUCH;
but then, if one scheme
OF HAPPINESS FAILS, HUMAN
nature turns to another.

—*JANE AUSTEN*
MANSFIELD PARK, 1814

Q
_____

DEAR JANE,

I FEEL LIKE MY BOYFRIEND WOULD

like me better as a blonde.

SHOULD I DYE MY HAIR?

A

WOMAN IS FINE FOR HER OWN
SATISFACTION ALONE. NO MAN WILL
ADMIRE HER THE MORE,
NO WOMAN WILL LIKE HER
THE BETTER FOR IT.

—JANE AUSTEN
NORTHANGER ABBEY, 1818

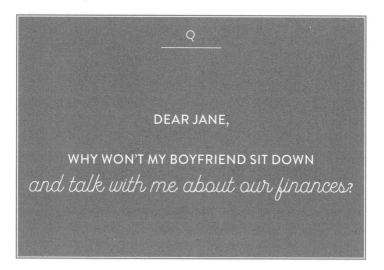

Q

DEAR JANE,

WHY WON'T MY BOYFRIEND SIT DOWN
and talk with me about our finances?

A

---

if there is anything
DISAGREEABLE GOING ON,
men are always
SURE TO GET OUT OF IT.

—*JANE AUSTEN*
PERSUASION, 1817

Q

DEAR JANE,

my boyfriend is really flighty—
I FEEL LIKE I PUT IN ALL THE EFFORT
and he reaps all the rewards.

A

TO FLATTER AND FOLLOW OTHERS,
without being flattered and
FOLLOWED IN TURN, IS BUT A STATE
of half enjoyment.

—*JANE AUSTEN*
PERSUASION, 1817

Q
___

DEAR JANE,

I WANT TO TRY

dating another girl,

BUT I'M AFRAID PEOPLE WON'T GET IT.

A

one half of the world
CANNOT UNDERSTAND
the pleasures of the other.

—JANE AUSTEN
EMMA, 1815

continues ➡➡

A
___

HE, WHO WILL NOT REASON,

IS A BIGOT;

HE, WHO CANNOT, IS A FOOL;

AND HE, WHO DARES NOT, IS A SLAVE.

—SIR WILLIAM DRUMMOND
ACADEMICAL QUESTIONS, 1805

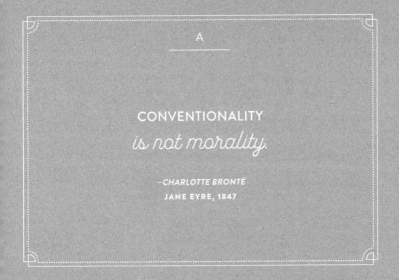

A

CONVENTIONALITY

is not morality.

—*CHARLOTTE BRONTË*
JANE EYRE, 1847

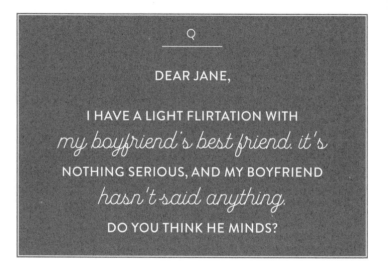

Q

DEAR JANE,

I HAVE A LIGHT FLIRTATION WITH *my boyfriend's best friend. it's* NOTHING SERIOUS, AND MY BOYFRIEND *hasn't said anything.* DO YOU THINK HE MINDS?

A

no man is offended
BY ANOTHER MAN'S ADMIRATION OF
the woman he loves.

—*JANE AUSTEN*
NORTHANGER ABBEY, 1818

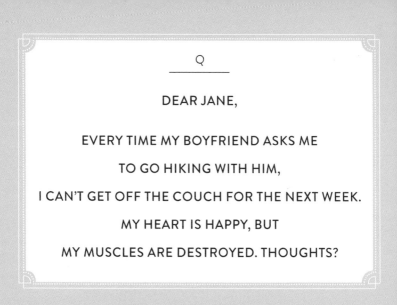

Q

DEAR JANE,

EVERY TIME MY BOYFRIEND ASKS ME
TO GO HIKING WITH HIM,
I CAN'T GET OFF THE COUCH FOR THE NEXT WEEK.
MY HEART IS HAPPY, BUT
MY MUSCLES ARE DESTROYED. THOUGHTS?

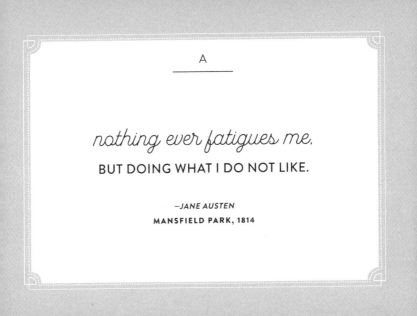

A

nothing ever fatigues me,
BUT DOING WHAT I DO NOT LIKE.

—*JANE AUSTEN*
MANSFIELD PARK, 1814

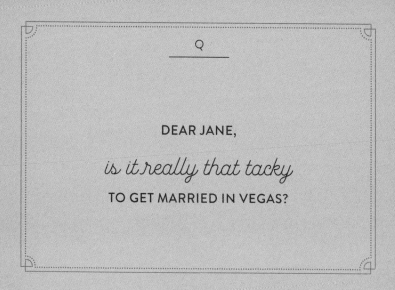

Q

DEAR JANE,

is it really that tacky

TO GET MARRIED IN VEGAS?

A

HAPPINESS IN MARRIAGE

is entirely a matter of chance.

—*JANE AUSTEN*
PRIDE AND PREJUDICE, 1813

Q

DEAR JANE,

how do I know

IF I'M IN LOVE?

A

I SUPPOSE THERE MAY BE

a hundred different ways

OF BEING IN LOVE.

—*JANE AUSTEN*
EMMA, 1815

BREAKUPS

Q

DEAR JANE,

I JUST GOT DUMPED,
and now I feel like
EVERYONE PITIES ME.

those who do not complain

ARE NEVER PITIED.

—*JANE AUSTEN*
PRIDE AND PREJUDICE, 1813

Q

DEAR JANE,

MY BOYFRIEND CHEATED ON ME WITH *my best friend . . . and now* THEY'RE DATING! THEY'RE BOTH TERRIBLE. *why do they get to be happy* WHILE I SUFFER?

A
───────

HOW LITTLE OF PERMANENT HAPPINESS

COULD BELONG TO A COUPLE

WHO WERE ONLY BROUGHT TOGETHER

BECAUSE THEIR PASSIONS WERE STRONGER

THAN THEIR VIRTUE.

—*JANE AUSTEN*
PRIDE AND PREJUDICE, 1813

continues ⟫

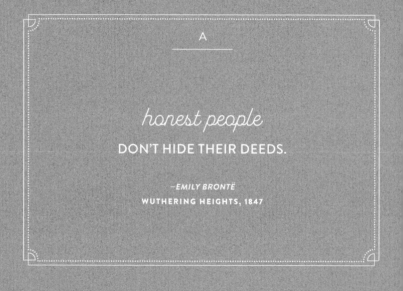

A

honest people

DON'T HIDE THEIR DEEDS.

—EMILY BRONTË

WUTHERING HEIGHTS, 1847

A

A MISTRESS NEVER IS
nor can be a friend.

—*LORD BYRON*
1788–1824

Q

DEAR JANE,

I THINK I'M STILL

attracted to my ex.

A
_____

THAT WOULD BE THE GREATEST MISFORTUNE

of all! —to find a man agreeable

WHOM ONE IS DETERMINED TO HATE!

—JANE AUSTEN
PRIDE AND PREJUDICE, 1813

continues ▶▶

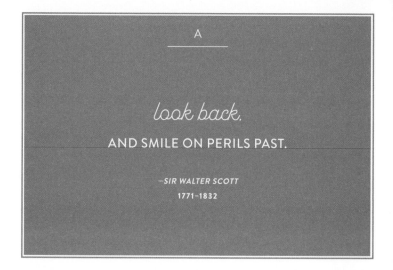

A

look back,

AND SMILE ON PERILS PAST.

—*SIR WALTER SCOTT*
1771–1832

FEAR NOT THE FUTURE,

weep not for the past.

—PERCY BYSSHE SHELLEY
THE REVOLT OF ISLAM, 1817

Q

DEAR JANE,

now that my relationship is over,

I FEEL BAD WHEN I REMEMBER

the good times.

A

THINK ONLY OF THE PAST

as its remembrance

GIVES YOU PLEASURE.

—*JANE AUSTEN*
PRIDE AND PREJUDICE, 1813

continues ➤➤

A

adversity is

THE FIRST PATH TO TRUTH.

—LORD BYRON

DON JUAN, 1824

A

SORROW IS KNOWLEDGE,
those that know the most
MUST MOURN THE DEEPEST.

—LORD BYRON
MANFRED, 1817

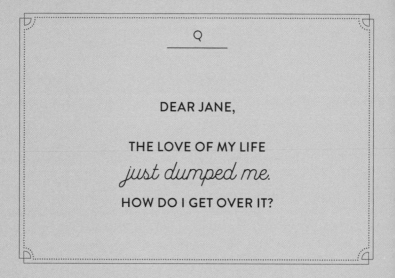

Q

DEAR JANE,

THE LOVE OF MY LIFE

just dumped me.

HOW DO I GET OVER IT?

A

time will generally
LESSEN THE INTEREST OF
every attachment
NOT WITHIN THE DAILY CIRCLE.

—*JANE AUSTEN*
EMMA, 1815

Q

DEAR JANE,

I JUST GOT DUMPED,

and I feel awful.

WHAT SHOULD I DO?

A

___

FRIENDSHIP IS CERTAINLY

the finest balm

FOR THE PANGS OF

disappointed love.

—*JANE AUSTEN*
NORTHANGER ABBEY, 1818

WELLNESS

Q
_____

DEAR JANE,

how do I cure a hangover?

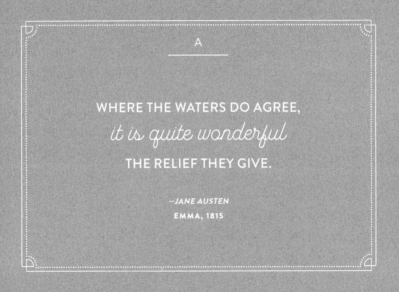

A

WHERE THE WATERS DO AGREE,
it is quite wonderful
THE RELIEF THEY GIVE.

—*JANE AUSTEN*
EMMA, 1815

Q

DEAR JANE,

I'M THINKING ABOUT DELETING
my facebook page.
THOUGHTS?

A

NOT KEEP A JOURNAL! . . . HOW ARE YOUR VARIOUS DRESSES TO BE REMEMBERED, AND THE PARTICULAR STATE OF YOUR COMPLEXION, AND CURL OF YOUR HAIR TO BE DESCRIBED IN ALL THEIR DIVERSITIES?

—*JANE AUSTEN*
NORTHANGER ABBEY, 1818

continues ➤➤

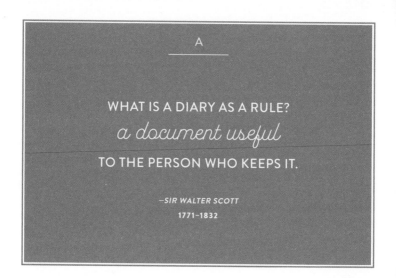

A

WHAT IS A DIARY AS A RULE?
a document useful
TO THE PERSON WHO KEEPS IT.

—SIR WALTER SCOTT
1771–1832

A

I'M JUST GOING TO WRITE

because I cannot help it.

—*CHARLOTTE BRONTË*

1816–1855

Q

DEAR JANE,

I AM NOT A GYM BUNNY,
but I keep thinking about
RUNNING A MARATHON. SHOULD I?

A

WHERE SOME DEGREE OF

strength of mind is given,

IT IS NOT A FEEBLE BODY

which will excuse us—

OR INCLINE US TO EXCUSE OURSELVES.

—*JANE AUSTEN*

SANDITON, 1817

Q

DEAR JANE,

why do they keep remaking

PRIDE AND PREJUDICE

when the Colin Firth/Jennifer Ehle

MINISERIES EXISTS?

A

perfection should not

HAVE COME QUITE SO SOON.

—JANE AUSTEN

EMMA, 1815

Q

DEAR JANE,

I stayed in bed

UNTIL 3 P.M. TODAY

and ate cereal.

IS THAT BAD?

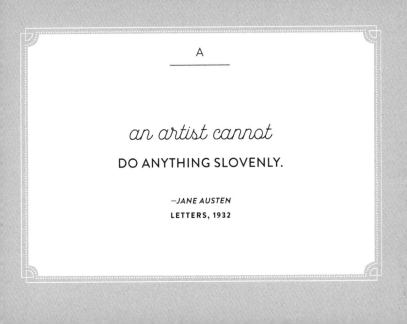

A

an artist cannot

DO ANYTHING SLOVENLY.

—*JANE AUSTEN*
LETTERS, 1932

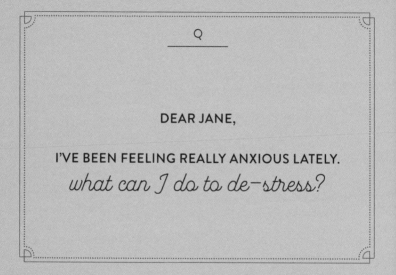

Q
_____

DEAR JANE,

I'VE BEEN FEELING REALLY ANXIOUS LATELY.
what can I do to de-stress?

A

AN INTERVAL OF MEDITATION,
serious and grateful,
WAS THE BEST CORRECTIVE
of everything dangerous.

—*JANE AUSTEN*
PERSUASION, 1817

continues ➤➤

A

ALWAYS LAUGH WHEN YOU CAN.

it is cheap medicine.

—*LORD BYRON*

1788–1824

A

a ruffled mind

MAKES A RESTLESS PILLOW.

—*CHARLOTTE BRONTË*
THE PROFESSOR, 1857

Q

DEAR JANE,

WHAT DO YOU RECOMMEND

for ennui?

A

every moment has its

PLEASURE AND ITS HOPE.

—JANE AUSTEN

MANSFIELD PARK, 1814

Q
___

DEAR JANE,

what's your

FAVORITE FITNESS ROUTINE?

A
_____

RUN MAD AS OFTEN AS YOU CHOOSE,

but do not faint.

–*JANE AUSTEN*
LOVE AND FREINDSHIP [SIC], 1790

Q
___

DEAR JANE,

AM I A LOSER IF I WANT TO

just stay in on friday

AND WATCH THE BBC?

A
_____

THERE IS NOTHING LIKE STAYING AT HOME

for real comfort.

—*JANE AUSTEN*
EMMA, 1815

continues ➤➤

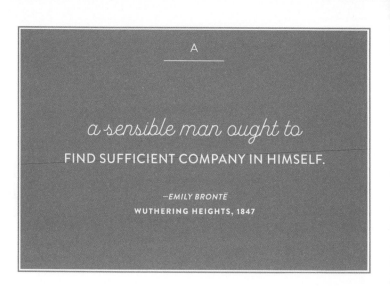

A

a sensible man ought to
FIND SUFFICIENT COMPANY IN HIMSELF.

—EMILY BRONTË
WUTHERING HEIGHTS, 1847

A

I ONLY GO OUT TO GET ME A

fresh appetite for being alone.

—*LORD BYRON*
JOURNAL

Q
_____

DEAR JANE,

I JUST FINISHED THE SHOW I WAS

binge watching on Netflix.

ANY RECOMMENDATIONS?

A

HOW MUCH SOONER
one tires of anything
THAN OF A BOOK!

—*JANE AUSTEN*
PRIDE AND PREJUDICE, 1813

Q

DEAR JANE,

my computer just crashed.

IS MY LIFE OVER?

A
───────

THERE SEEMS SOMETHING MORE

SPEAKINGLY INCOMPREHENSIBLE IN

THE POWERS, THE FAILURES, THE

INEQUALITIES OF MEMORY, THAN IN ANY

OTHER OF OUR INTELLIGENCES.

—JANE AUSTEN
MANSFIELD PARK, 1814

Q

DEAR JANE,

I'VE BEEN FEELING
a bit fatigued of late.
WHAT WOULD YOU RECOMMEND?

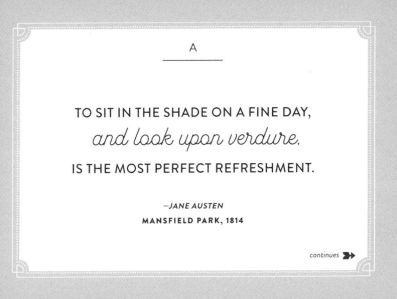

A
_____

TO SIT IN THE SHADE ON A FINE DAY,

and look upon verdure,

IS THE MOST PERFECT REFRESHMENT.

—*JANE AUSTEN*

MANSFIELD PARK, 1814

continues ➤➤

A
_____

THERE IS A PLEASURE IN THE PATHLESS WOODS,

THERE IS A RAPTURE ON THE LONELY

SHORE, THERE IS SOCIETY WHERE NONE INTRUDES,

BY THE DEEP SEA, AND MUSIC IN ITS ROAR;

I LOVE NOT MAN THE LESS, BUT NATURE MORE.

—LORD BYRON
CHILDE HAROLD'S PILGRIMAGE, 1818

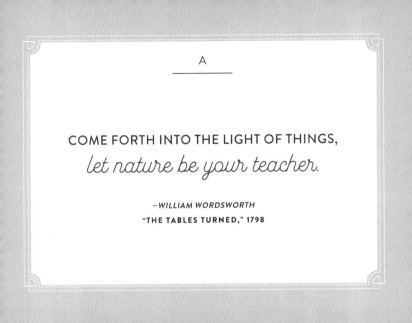

A

COME FORTH INTO THE LIGHT OF THINGS,
let nature be your teacher.

—*WILLIAM WORDSWORTH*
"THE TABLES TURNED," 1798

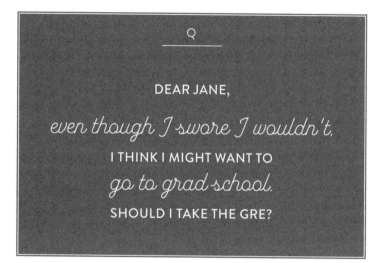

Q

DEAR JANE,

even though I swore I wouldn't,

I THINK I MIGHT WANT TO

go to grad school.

SHOULD I TAKE THE GRE?

A

HOW WONDERFUL, HOW VERY WONDERFUL,
the operations of time,
AND THE CHANGES OF THE HUMAN MIND!

—JANE AUSTEN
MANSFIELD PARK, 1814

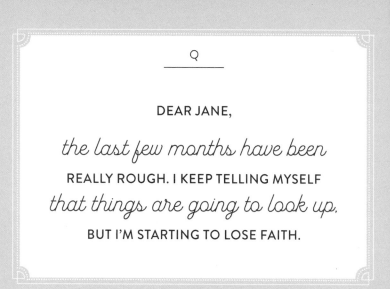

Q
_____

DEAR JANE,

the last few months have been

REALLY ROUGH. I KEEP TELLING MYSELF

that things are going to look up,

BUT I'M STARTING TO LOSE FAITH.

A
_____

IF THINGS ARE GOING

untowardly one month,

THEY ARE SURE TO MEND THE NEXT.

—*JANE AUSTEN*

EMMA, 1815